Poetry 'n That

S.G. McCloskey

COPYRIGHT PROTECTION WARNING

The author has registered this work at ProtectMyWork.com

Published By

Celtic New Dawn Press

"This collection of short poems cover a diverse array of topics, discussing Brexit, Theresa May's time as prime minister, Scottish independence, and the plight of the downtrodden during Christmas over the course of its pages.

The author approaches politics, love, sex, and social expectations candidly...The poems discuss politics with little appreciation for the monarchy or Tory government, though they seem designed to make the poetic messages as enjoyable as possible without watering down the author's convictions, to where the focus is more on change than on blaming the voters...

...The poems have a generally positive tone, though poignant at times, especially when discussing the glory of Scotland and how things have changed since the nation became part of Great Britain. Overall, the collection is life affirming, urging readers to have a positive outlook on humanity at large, though it deprecates the actions of the elite 1% with a decidedly satirical flair...

...Readers who enjoy the heartfelt observations and opinions of an outspoken artist will enjoy these poems. They're vibrant, colorful, and culturally-sensitive while reflecting upon universal ideas like freedom, life, and love."

- *The Book Review Directory*

Disclaimer:

This poetry collection contains profanity language, descriptions of sexual activity and also highlights some issues that some readers may find offensive. Please do not purchase or read if any of these personally offend you. As the works are aimed at an adult audience, please ensure you are over 18+ years old before purchasing, reading or sharing with your peer group. The views and opinions expressed are entirely those of the author alone and do not represent the views or opinions of any political or activist groups, parties, clubs or movements.

Dedication:

This collection of poetry works is dedicated to the outsiders, the truth-seekers and those who think outside the box marked 'normal.'

Introduction:

Having released a few short collections of poems previously, I finally decided to 'throw everything into one bag' and release the total sum of my poetic works in one book. Within these pages, I've worked from personal to political, national to international and transgender to transcender issues. As a few poems are written in purely Scots dialect, I've included a handy glossary of terms (English translation) pertaining to these. At least a quarter of the works presented are previously unpublished, making it right up-to-date in terms of my written creativity. I hope you might enjoy reading it all.

slainte mhor,

Seána Geri McCloskey, 2018

Contents:

THE WOMAN WITHIN

The woman within is waking up,
She's been asleep too long -
The woman within is wide awake,
Whether she's right or wrong -

The woman within is waking up,
Long memories remain -
The woman within is wide awake,
She's broke the locks and chains -

The woman within is all dressed up,
And sees her own true self -
The woman within looks gorgeous now,
In fine spirit and good health -

The woman within yearns to be free,
She's a sister and mother too -
The woman within is not a freak,
She's just like me and you -

The woman within is breaking out,
She grows stronger by the day -
The woman within is only love,
She'll show you come what may –

SOMEBODY ELSE'S WEAN AND ME

Somebody else's wean and me,
Are lying here again,
He's been to the park,
It's getting after dark,
Time to sleep now, ma wee friend -

Somebody else's wean and me,
Are lying here again,
He's learning to talk,
And soon he will walk,
His life's an adventure each day -

Somebody else's wean and me,
Are lying here again,
His life is carefree,
But still he can see,
The space where Mama used to be -

Somebody else's wean and me,
Are lying here again,
The sperm donor's disappeared,
Must be too f*cking feart,
To face up to my little friend -

Somebody else's wean and me,
Are lying here again,
If it wisnae fir me, an Orphan he'd be,
He's under my wing and he's free -

Somebody else's wean and me,
Are lying here again,
If you don't miss him,
He's got brothers and sister,
He's one of us now, can't you see?

2

WHITE PICKET FENCE DREAM

White picket fence dream,
Smashed to smithereens,
And scattered all across the ground,
With the schrill of the hollow wind,
The only haunting sound -

Like a ghost of yesteryear,
All swept away my dear,
You had everything had you known it,
It wasn't me that's blown it -

Thinking of winter nights,
When the kids were snugged up tight,
In the night garden on tv,
These are my memories -

Swing-parks, shops and more,
Late walks upon the shore,
Trips across the nation,
Passing through Largs railway station -

Foundations of a dream,
To build on as a team,
Layed strong enough by one,
This team will carry on -

And all who played their part,
You know it in your heart,
What the future held for six we'ans you didn't think,
When you bought their Mama another drink –

It was all for "fun and laughs,"
You must think I'm f*cking daft,
If I didn'ae guess what she was daeing,
Or in who else's bed she lays in -

You might think you got clean away,
But just wait 'til another day,
When your karma comes a-calling,
It's your own picket fence that will be falling -

I would try to save you from the misery,
That has been wrongly wrecked upon me,
But that's impossible you'll see,
Karma takes it debt times three -

And from a partnership's demise,
A broken marriage funeral pyre,
Scatter the ashes on the wind,
The Phoenix will arise...

A WOMAN'S WORK

A woman's work is never done,
Even with the setting of the sun,
Sometimes that work has just begun,
Fir home and hearth and love -

A woman's work just never ends,
She's got no time tae be with friends,
She works for something that transcends,
Fir we'ans and family -

Washing in and washing oot,
She knows what it's really all a'boot,
To cook and clean all roond-a-boot,
Fir home and hearth and love -

While the time bell rings and drinks go doon,
In the alehouses of yer local toon,
She's working away like a midnight loon,
Fir we'ans and family -

When the sun comes up as a golden rule,
She'll see the we'ans go aff tae school,
Clean and tidy and nobody's fool,
Fir home and hearth and love -

YE CANNAE WEAR YER SISTER'S CLAES

Ye cannae wear yer sister's claes,
D'ye want the whole toon tae think yer gay?
Disnae metter if ye just like silk and lace,
Ye just cannae wear yer sister's claes -

Yer sister and her pals wear make-up and stuff,
Skimpy tops, jewellery and silly wee skirts,
Silk stockings, heels and lacy trim cuffs,
You'd love to look that pretty, is that asking too much?

She looks so sweet, dressed up in a frock,
You'd love to wear one tae, but people would mock,
They'd slander ye daft wi' their gossip and talk,
And if they could, throw ye right in the dock -

The judge in his chair with a big wig and gown,
Would hear the prosecution with a bluidy deep frown,
Of how ye became, the talk o' the town,
"That's enough o' that son, you're going down!"

You could deal drugs and that would be okay,
Get done fir drunk driving and come what may,
You'll be forgiven fir 'aw that, one of these days,
But ye just cannae wear yer sister's claes!

BREATHE

Breathe,
Breathe me in,
It's not a sin,
If it's not Sunday,
Anyday could be fun day -

Smell,
Smell my scent,
From August to Lent,
There's no charge or no rent,
It's just heaven sent -

Touch,
Touch me soon,
Tomorrow's too late,
I'd be too out-of-date,
And heaven can wait -

Kiss,
Kiss me now,
With your wild, hungry lips,
In long and short sips,
While the veil of love slips -

Taste,
Taste me good,
Just like you should,
Surrender your power,
To this wild mountain flower –

Suck,
Suck me strong,
Lick me good,
Suck me long,
There's no right or no wrong –

Give,
Give me your sex,
I don't need a text,
You won't get a hex,
Just give me your sex -

Cream,
Give me your cream,
Like a f*cking wet dream,
From Shakespeare's last scene,
Just give me your cream -

Hug,
Hug like you know,
In love's afterglow,
It wasn't a show,
I meant it, you know -

NOWHERE STREET

Nobody wandered Nowhere street,

As the snow was falling fast -

While the brass band blasted loudly,

Like the ghost of Xmas past –

Their army of salvation,

Really had a plan,

While a homeless junkie vagrant,

Searched through a garbage can –

Soon the light was fading.

Darkness crept in all around -

The wail of a Police siren,

Was the only sound –

And standing in the shadows,

Like Mary Magdalene -

She watched the cars cruise by,

Hoping to sell sin –

She stepped into the dim street light,

Wondering who would stop and stare?

And who would gaze in wonder?

And who would pay her fare?

While a taxi driver waited,

Outside the mansion house -

To take a mistress home,

Leaving a master to his spouse –

As the junkie popped another vein,

And took another hit -

The north wind sold its freezing cold,

But he never felt a bit –

The children slept so soundly,

In the houses in the ring -

Waiting for Santa Klause,

And all that he would bring –

Nobody smiled and thought of them,

With their faces full of joy -

The tearing of the wrapping,

Unveils a favorite toy –

And somewhere in the distance,

Waiting for New Year,

Moving in between two worlds,

An Angel shed a tear -

F*CK THE FRACKERS

F*ck the frackers,
They're pure f*cking crackers,
Of the 1% Elite,
And their Tory backers -

They're all fly-by-night,
You heard me right,
Out for a fast buck,
They'll tell you any old $h*te -

Like Fracking is clean,
There's no danger at all,
Tell that to the people,
Who's lives went to the wall -

The water is poisoned,
There's a sea of dead fish,
The plants have all died,
So stop talking p*sh -

You sound like a drone,
Having a moan,
About the new age protectors,
In the fracking zone -

People before profit,
Don't be a rocket,
You're killing the planet,
Have you finally got it?

TOXIC LITTLE TORIES

Experts, sexperts,
And outright f*cking perverts,
Maybot's, new laws,
Descending into chaos -
State hacked, freshly fracked,
Tracked from here and there and back -
Steam me, ream me,
F*ck me over 'til you've creamed me,
Toxic little Tories, sitting in a row -

Sectioned and sanctioned,
By someone in a mansion,
Smart city, smart life,
Go and tell yer f*cking wife -
Rape Clause, nae baws,
May as well chop them off -
At two we'ans, quit playing,
Whit the f*ck d'ye think yer daeing?
In every street, in every town,
We'll keep the population down -
Toxic little Tories, sitting in a row -

Nerve gas, free pass,
Into Porton Down at last,
Bad Vlad, he must be mad,
He made the Daily Mail so sad -
Nae greetin,' nae cheatin,'
Except at the Privy Council meetings,
Rebel guns, in the sun,
This will be so much fun,
On the make and on the take,
From everyone called Daniel Blake –

The bombs drop, they will not stop,
'Til they've got the f*cking lot,
When the price of oil is at stake,
Imperialist excuses can't sound fake,
Toxic little Tories, sitting in a row -

So sniff a line of Prince Charles,
The King once three years have passed,
Of royal blood, there is no doubt,
As another Windsor knocks one out -
Feeding frenzy, in the press,
Forget about the Tory mess,
They'll have to pin, Kate's perma-grin,
To a poster on each council bin,
It must be great, the tourists smile,
Living in the British Isles?
Toxic little Tories, sitting in a row –

ODE TAE TUNNOCKS

Tunnocks, oh Tunnocks,
Ma heart's in a flummox,
Yer biscuits wance wir Scottish,
But now they're not-ish -
And that tastes bitter-sweet,
In aw' oor mouths & stomachs -

Can ye tell us 'aw tae where,
The Lion Rampant ran?
When ye sold yer brand new biscuits,
Tae somewhere in Japan?
In the big empty space,
Where the Scottish Lion lay,
There's a bluidy union flag,
And he's been replaced -

A biscuit's just a biscuit,
And a flag is just a flag,
But there's more tae this,
And some have missed,
The 'Better Together' tag -

Another Rampant sell-out,
From another millionaire,
Who played with Scottish politics,
So he could sell his wares -

If you go down tae the underground,
In dear old London Town,
Have a look around and ye cannae miss it -
Tunnocks is now a 'Great British' company,
That really takes the biscuit!

SEX BOTS

The sex bots are on the rampage,
Spreading like wildfire in the digital age,
Get them on Facebook, Twitter and Instagram,
Have a chat on What's App, that's the plan -

She's got a fake tan and designer t*ts,
But if you really saw her, you'd just be in bits,
That's her 'real' photograph, don't cha know?
She's a cross between Beyoncé & Marilyn Monroe -

She's a pole swinging, lap dancin' digital doll,
She's a church going, home baking, bad-ass gangster's
moll,
If you really want to bang her up against a wall?
She'll do it by request, streaming live and all -

She's a Russian supermodel, who lives in Paisley,
But if you ask her straight, she's never heard of Fagey,
But string along with it, cos it's all the ragey,
You've got 15 mutual friends, so it's not that cagey -

Would you like to see her strip, wear handcuffs or
skinny dipping?
Or wear something else that you think is fitting?
If the price is right, she'll surely be submitting,
Just read between the lines that are never written –

TO THE GREAT DELUDED

Wee, sleekit, tim'rous Scotland In Union,
Ah tell ye right noo, that's a good yin -
For Scotland's freedom, they've tried tae scupper,
But they hae the bluidy cheek, tae hae a Burn's Supper!

Scots wha hae wi' Wallace bled,
But these hoodwinked clowns, they are in bed -
With the 1% Elite and the English queen,
Delusion like this has ne'r been seen -

Except on the turncoats who ran at Falkirk,
Except on John Menteith, who gave up Wallace -
Except on the Campbell's turning at Glencoe,
Except on Toom Tabard, the king of empty coats -

This is land is our land, it's yours and mine,
But ah tell once again, there's no reason or rhyme -
They must be drinking from a barrel or too much wine,
Wha think they can be Scottish and British, at the same
time!

THE BRAVE MEN OF BUTE

The Brave Men of Bute,
Took the fastest route,
O'er water, field & forest,
To stand with William Wallace -

Six hundred men,
Marching through the glen,
'Tis doubteful we'll see,
Their likes again -

On the Faw Kirk's field,
They refused to yield,
In the year 1298,
They marched to their fate -

When John Stewart fell,
Almost into death's knell,
They wid not forsake him,
And they covered him well -

With a ring of steel,
Like a schiltron's shield,
They stood as a Clan,
To the very last man -

One by one they fell,
Into bluidy death's knell,
The Brave Men of Bute,
We remember them well!

THE RULES OF DIVISION

Divide and Rule,
It's a favorite tool,
Of the British State,
Handed down on a plate -

Division in schools,
Geniuses and fools,
Who'll get a degree,
Just wait and see -

Division in work,
All round like Friar Tuck,
Keep them in competition,
With no chance of remission -

Division by wealth,
Done like nuclear stealth,
Corrosive to the core,
Then divide some more -

Division by Royals,
Never share their spoils,
If you're blood ain't blue,
Get to the back of the queue -

Division by Religion,
With Sectarian precision,
To split a people in two,
Turns me against you -

Division by Gender,
That's another mind bender,
Boy or girl it seems,
And anyone in-between –

Division by class,
Is division en masse,
Keeps us right in our place,
Then divide by Race -

Division by Race,
Like a slap in the face,
But beneath the skin it's said,
We all bleed red -

Division by ethnic origin,
Like a visit from the Morrigan,
Is the death of inclusion,
As too many get excluded -

As long as we're divided,
The State has decided,
That's the way it should be,
Divided you and me –

THE PRICE OF FREEDOM

The price of freedom is so high,
In the past men had to die -
Or suffer terribly or deny,
Or pay the price of treason -

Egos grew and some collided,
The state just loves a movement divided -
Once the call fir freedom has subsided,
There is nae rhyme or reason -

You on the stage give nothing more,
Than the guy at the back who joins the roar -
And the lady who goes round the doors,
In any weather or season -

So let the singer sing his sang,
And let the speaker tak' fir lang -
Stand togither an' we'll make a big bang,
If there's nae mair room, just squeeze in -

The key to unlock a Unicorn's chain,
Isnae in a single name -
Or a party, group or in growing disdain,
It's in you and me and reason -

Hear the Stone of Destiny,
It whispers quiet to set you free -
Let's walk togither, you and me,
They cannae dae us 'aw fir treason!

THE POWERS THAT BE

The powers that be,
Are all found to be,
So near and so far,
In olde Temple Bar -

A state that's inside,
Another state so wide,
The 99 percent can wait,
But can't penetrate -

In an old square mile,
Dressed in grandeur's style -
City within city,
Tarted up, but not pretty -

P2, who knew,
What 2 stones could do,
Swinging cold as a fridge,
Beneath Blackfriar's bridge -

The newspapers moaned,
The Vatican groaned,
While the lawyers spread cheese,
But kept talking legalese -

In their own special language,
The 1% sandwich,
Known only to them,
And not common men –

Independence Day pie,
And the 4th of July,
We'll never know why,
Freedom passed us all by -

Stitched up in their laws,
We're clutching at stars,
The Bar & the Crown,
They've got it locked down -

The UK plc
And Washington DC,
We're employees you'll see,
Not just you and me -

Not the words of some old bint,
We've all done our stint,
Your eyes they might squint,
It's in the small print -

In LEGAL FICTION names,
They've got us all framed,
Half the world it got maimed,
And the Unicorn tamed -

From cradle to grave,
The ploughman, the knave,
There's none they don't own,
By crown copyright & loans.

ODE TO OLDE FRIENDS

Picture postcards in a row,
Fly through my memory -
Thinking of old times you know,
When Johnny was the DJ -

To mix it up and include rock,
Wasn't always easy -
But only when, the clock struck ten,
It all fell in so freely -

My lazer lights were outta sight,
And batteries ran the sound -
The bass bins flinched and Billy whinged,
With the levels that I found -

Big Jamie was the bouncer man,
And Phil worked on the bar -
As Johnny rocked the joint each night,
Everybody was a star -

Equality days, you'd be amazed,
As the rich man drank with those on the dole -
They laughed out loud, their eyes popped out,
As the lassies twirled 'roon the dancing pole -

But the music rocked, around the clock,
As we drank the Clachan dry -
To 'purple haze' we were not fazed,
And sometimes touched the sky –

The highs and lows, we reached you know,
Sometimes they were a sin -
We ran out o' beer, one new year,
Then took Murray hame in a wheelie bin -
We're getting older and bless the soldier,
The wee man's not around -
Those days to recall, when I think of you all,
Can be triggered by a sound -

Remembering you, Blink 182,
I miss you like a song -
Highway to Hell, Division Bell,
Whether we were right or wrong -

To do it all again once more,
Well, that would be so great -
If it's not to be, 'tween you and me,
"I'll see you in the next world, don't be late!"

The good times, the bad times,
Were all only glad times,
Something to be shared and measured -
Against the trouble and strife, of daily life,
Those days are only treasured ...

THE TOLLING OF THE BELL

DUP-licitiy is rife,
But that's just f*cking life -
And the puppet politicians,
Won't be thinking twice -

To get Britannia in a war,
And settle an old score -
For the peasants are revolting,
Everyday, just more and more -

Despite the Daily Mail,
Brexit's still a fail -
Little England's wanton wailing,
Is just beyond the pale -

And the deal's near stitched and done,
By the Toxic Tory scum -
But the future isn't orange,
And YES ain't on the run -

And Plaid are still alive,
So are the forty-five -
Just get the popcorn out,
As sterling takes a dive -

But Harry's spurned the throne,
He's not a f*cking drone -
As he knows Britannia,
Will soon be all alone -

He knows what it's about,
In the stampede to get out -
Of this blasted, bluidy union,
Of that there is no doubt -

We fought them on the beaches,
We fought them in the air -
But just like Winston's old cigars,
UK's beyond repair -

If it served its purpose well,
Only time will tell -
Tick-tock until it falls apart,
Hear the tolling of the bell...

PEOPLE BEFORE PROFIT

People before profit,
Have you 1% Elite muppets finally got it?
Somehow we kinda doubt it,
And soon we're gonna shout it -

We'll stand together in defiance,
Of a Toxic Tory alliance -
It's just not rocket science,
No more right-wing appliance -

People's lives they were at stake,
While the profiteers were on the make -
And the politicians gave in like flakes,
So this is what it takes -

A terrible tragedy to befall,
Seen by one and all -
The writing was on the wall,
But fell on deaf ears if you recall?

We're not taking this anymore,
You'll hear the people roar -
With one voice we will soar,
And turn our backs on you,
Peacefully forever more ...

ODE TO THERESA MAYHEM

Theresa Mayhem,
Whit ye gonnie dae hen?
Brexit means exit,
The UK told ye wi' a big pen -

Strong & stable,
Meant 'willing not able' -
Soundbites & stage-fright,
It wiz aw' a big fable -

Corbyn 'the commie',
Could be friends wi' Johnny,
If he let's Scotland vote,
On oor own future zonie -

But Theresa's in trouble,
And big soapy bubble -
Boris & the boys,
Are aw' up tae sumthin' -

The EU are laughing,
UKIP's teeth ir nashin' -
As Theresa's shoes,
Hiv went right oot o' fashion -

She rolled the dice,
And took a chance -
But her lucky 13,
Failed wi' nae romance –

But the 99%,
Won't give up the fight,
We'll be back to reclaim,
Oor ain human rights -

When you next see Theresa,
Under any lights -
She'll be p*shed in the street,
And jaked oot her tights -

It was all a game,
And aw' a gamble -
And that's the end,
'O Theresa's ramble ...

SO WHO VOTED TORY?

So who voted Tory?
It's the same old sorry story -
The traitors in this country,
In all their feckin' glory -

Theresa is in the huffit,
Just like little Miss Muffit -
She disnae see the danger,
Is hanging on so worth it?

Along came a spider,
And sat down beside her -
Her name's Arlene & she's the queen,
Of the new Red Hand Commando -

It's like an early bereavement,
For the Good Friday Agreement -
They've set it on fire,
Like a funeral pyre,
And nobody seems to see it -

They said Corbyn was a sympathizer,
But Theresa's a good disguiser -
When she went to bed, with the DUP red,
Just for an appetizer -

You reap just what you sow,
The main course is a bitter blow -
She'll hiv tae defend, and play pretend,
'Til the end of auld Britannia ...

WEE RUTH THE MOOTH

Wee Ruth the Mooth Davidson,
Should go live in Evasham,
But I wouldn't wish it on any of them,
They don't deserve such total mayhem -

When she's not sitting on a gun,
She's likes her photo done,
With her Orange Order cronies,
That's how elections run -

In this day & age,
It's an utter outrage,
To bring this disgrace,
That should be on the front page -

To local politics,
They'll find any cap that fits,
With their policies in bits,
If any ever did exist -

Except for "stop the SNP",
And the school meals for free,
And block the referenda,
'Til they all have senile dementia -

But they misjudged the forty-five,
We're kicking & alive,
For indie we will strive,
As Brexit takes a dive –

So tell Theresa May,
You've wasted all yer pay,
'Cos Ruthie has no say,
We'll see her off one day -

Like Kim Jong-un's twin,
It would really be a sin,
To wish her on anyone,
Who hasn't done a thing –

FOR WHAT DIED THE SONS OF SCOTIA?

For what died the sons of Scotia?
Was it greed?
That those very sons fight and bleed?
On the battlefields of 'ore,
Tell me, what was it for?
For a bunch of 'I'm alright union jacks' to vote Naw?

For what died the sons of Scotia?
Was it fame?
For what flowed Scotia's blood in rivers,
When Alexander chased the Dane -
And still breathes and is so alive,
In the sons and daughters of the forty-five -
And her heroes of yester-year who were slain.

For what died the sons of Scotia?
Was it greed?
That gave Wallace and Bruce the courage to lead,
And for their country did they not bleed?
The spider, the lion and the unicorn,
Have watched their nation's sovereignty torn -
From the hands of those to whom it belongs,
While the fat-cats and bankers laugh and scorn.

To whom do we owe our allegiance today?
If not to our heroes, Saxon's very bane -
To sterling, the euro or petro-dollar,
So that we can wear the collar
Of the slave?
To whom do we owe our allegiance today?

For what died the sons of Scotia?
Was it to live on an eternal banker's loan,
In an independent fracking zone?
To be spied on with cameras and drones?
Where is the freedom you may ask,
In producing a citizen's pass,
While the politicians hide behind masks,
With their soundbites and scripts that won't last.

For what died the sons of Scotia
by the Clan?
Where is the equality of man,
When it doesn't fit the 1% Elite masterplan -
Where is the meritocracy to be seen?
When some are born to privilege and greed,
And others to foodbanks and need.

For what died the sons of Scotia?

THE MEN IN SUITS

The men in suits are in cahoots,
They sit and talk all day -
Of laws and bribes, they dodge their wives,
And give themselves more pay -

They waffle here and waffle there,
How they'll sort it all for free -
They'll tax us less, to fix this mess,
Nothing's changed that I can see -

Must be our fate, living in this state,
Of daily unending war -
Just switch terrains, it's just the same,
What are we fighting for?

Guns and arms and arms and guns,
And profit to be made -
Bought and sold, for more black gold,
And laws to make us slaves -

Yes the men in suits are in cahoots,
They sit and talk all day -
But now we're wise, one day we'll rise,
And much to their dismay!

DON'T VOTE TORY

Don't vote Tory,
It's the same old story,
Like digging Thatcher up from the grave -

Strong & Stable,
That's another fable,
Chanted by the woman that's filling in for Dave -

She's not been elected,
It's time she was rejected,
Send her back to the 1% Elite -

Like the puppet she was,
Serving her masters cause,
Bring us news of her impending defeat -

It's all been stage managed,
But it does more damage,
Deception is all that it's for -

Soundbites & scripts,
Get repeated in blips,
Like a CD stuck in a drawer -

If ye know yer history,
There is no mystery,
In the so-called land of glory -

In the coming season,
There's just no valid reason,
Why anyone would want to vote Tory!

KEYBOARD WARRIORS ON THE RAMPAGE

Wonderful keyboard warriors,
Have a way of slipping out,
When someone puts up a real event,
And gives these c***s a shout -

Jimmy's got pneumonia,
But Joe's just got the flu,
Sheila's cat's stuck up a tree,
So tell me something new?

Davy works the weekends,
Says he'll see what he can do,
And Archie's got his ballet lessons,
Keep that between me & you -

Annie cannae find it on the map,
Her sat-nav's failing too -
Could somebody help her find a bus?
As Google's more than she can do -

So when a push comes to a shove,
You'd laugh and cry or sob,
To find there's only three of us,
Standing in this demo flash-mob -

They'll do anything for the cause,
Even take a bullet for you,
But where they are at your event?
No-one has a clue!

THE BLIGHTY MACHINE

In England & Wales
And the Yorkshire Dales,
How anyone votes Tory,
My mind f*cking fails -

But the news is so stale,
In the old Daily Mail,
"Corbyn's the bad guy,
He should be in jail!"

Just watch BBC,
While supping yer tea,
Subliminal programming,
They're experts you see -

"Brexit is good,
And Corbyn is bad,
UKIP are great,
They're more than a fad!"

So give them more space,
And Nigel's dumb face,
He's a joke in a suit,
And a f*cking disgrace -

Keep checking yer screens,
You won't see the Greens,
Or the bad SNP,
On the Blighty machine –

Come June the 8th,
With short-nails we wait,
If the Tories have won,
Tell me this is a dream -

Not one we'll escape from,
Nor the Butcher's Apron,
For another five years,
We're in for a jail term -

So read it & weep,
As you walk down the streets,
In the ghost of a country,
That's gone down the creek ...

THE SAME OLD STORY

Norman Tebbit,
Wants a sharp exit,
He'd get on his own bike,
Just for Brexit -
Sayin' "f*ck the EU nationals,
They can just forget it!"

He's not opposed to leaving,
Unlike Tarzan,
Who strangled his own dog,
Buried in the garden -
He brought down Thatcher,
The school milk snatcher,
Wearing a camouflage jacket,
While she drove a tank an' -

Gave everyone a dose of misery,
After closing down all the heavy industry,
As she waved a Union Flag with a thin veneer smile,
After punching Argentina in the Falkland Isles -

And old King Coal,
Went on the dole,
As Britain disappeared,
Down a financial black hole -
As the factory doors closed,
For the last time,
Leaving no future,
For yours and mine –

That's the trouble with the Tories,
Just join the dots,
Cause just like a leopard,
They don't change their spots -

So f*ck the Tories,
It's the same old story,
Of yet another 99% defeat,
And yet another win, for the 1% Elite...

CITIZENS NOT SLAVES

To the fraudsters, the bankers, the 1% w*nkers,
Hiding away from the sun -
In darkness they're counting, their ill-gotten mountains,
Of stolen gold, from everyone -

To fake politicians, there is no remission,
Your spin doctors spew out your lies -
Of off-shore accounts, tax haven amounts,
Of bullsh*t and pie-in-the-sky -

While we pay our rent, with nothing left spent,
Threadbare are our lives, on the run -
But listen now well, to the toll of the bell,
Your days are numbered and done -

By this decree, just wait and you'll see,
The dawn of democratic meritocracy -
Equality for all, your empires will fall,
The people will set themselves free -

There is no escape, from your own fate,
And karma will not be undone -
Citizens Not Slaves, will topple your knaves,
Tiocfaidh ár lá, Our Day Will Come –

WE ARE SISTERS AND WE ARE BROTHERS

Our pens will be our guns,
With keyboards full of fire -
Our words will simply stun,
As we expose the 1% liars -

Our banners will proclaim the truth,
We'll hold them ever higher -
And when the news gets blacked-out,
We'll stand firm and never tire -

There is no hiding place,
The truth will seek them out -
The 99 will have their day,
Of that there is no doubt -

Pantomime politics has had its day,
No more the two-horse race -
Now anyone's a politician,
Who wants to show their face -

Don't allow yourself to be sucked in,
By their divide and rule -
Cos under the skin we bleed the same,
Division is for fools -

We're upping up the anti,
And stepping up our game -
Now's the day & now's the hour,
Nothing will ever be the same -

So don't stand on the sidelines,
And leave it up to others -
Come and join the 99,
We are sisters and we are brothers!

THE OUTSIDERS

The queue for the latest gadget goes round the corner,
The homeless shiver when the cold wind bites -
But the outsiders will be the only ones,
Camping out here tomorrow night -

Greed has taken us to the brink,
Could we any further sink?
To call a Roma just a 'Tink,'
And acknowledge the lost with just a blink -

While feet do shuffle and elbows dig,
To grasp the latest tv so big -
Fights break out and shoppers attack,
Well saying this Friday was so black -

Not a number and not a name,
For this to happen is insane -
Paper cup dreams fall down by the score,
Like Oliver Twist they want some more -

Society pulls the Dodger's tricks,
As Fagin laughs within the mix -
And the soup kitchens open their doors once more,
As another Tory b*stard burns another score –

1936

Poor Adolf was astounded,
His worst fears were confounded -
When he fired the gun and bold Jesse won,
Then took the gold that was rounded -

This was a total disgrace,
Where was his master-race?
The Ayrans lost and much to their cost,
It wiped the smile right off his face -

With an unease in his tummy,
He fairly spat the dummy -
Then stormed off to bed,
With an aching head,
Due to everyone's blood being red -

He called up Himmler in the morning,
And slapped Josef Goebbels without warning -
Set Europe on fire,
Build a big funeral pyre,
And leave millions to their mourning –

BREXIT, LEG-IT, MAKE A SHARP EXIT

Brexit, Leg-it, make a sharp exit,
'cos Nigel don't want Romanians in the door that's next-
it,
The very idea has got him got him vexit -
So he changed the constitution, but never was elected

While Gove & Boris, played at being Chuck Norris,
Preaching dangerous times to anyone called Doris,
And the immigrants would soon be taking over
England's forests -
Propaganda on par with old George Soros -

So close all the borders and build a wall,
To keep out Donald Trump, make it ten feet tall,
And we don't want no bloody foreigners standing in the
hall,
That's too near the living-room, too close to call -

So make a Vauxhall car & then we'll park it,
Right outside the single European market,
Send Kate Middleton to reach the target,
With her fake perma-grin, Brussels will be smarted -

They have a master-plan, just wait and see,
To sell Frey Bentos pies & 'English tea',
If it came from China, who really cares?
They've got a family of Windsor's to sell their wares -

Poor old Philip's got a dodgy ticker,
Don't worry 'bout that, just use any Royal arse-licker,
B-list celebs queuing up by the score,
To sell England by the pound,
Who could ask for more?

Scotland, as it happens, never voted for it,
But as per usual, London will ignore it -
Where this is going, is anybody's guess?
We can only hope, the answer will be YES –

GOODBYE BRITANNIA

Goodbye Britannia,
You couldn't rule the waves -
Without the bonnie nation,
Named Scotland The Brave -

Our Gaelic, pipes & children,
No longer heard aloud -
Banned during Highland Clearances,
Buried in a tartan shroud -

On Culloden's bloody moor,
The bodies piled high -
Their sons you dressed in army clothes,
And sent them off to die -

In far off lands around the world,
You pillaged, raped & claimed -
Behind a Bluidy Union Flag,
You ought to be ashamed -

There is no hope and glory,
In all you have become -
At last your ship is sailing,
Into the sinking sun -

And from the ashes of this funeral pyre,
That burns before our eyes -
Just like the Phoenix is Reborn,
Scotland Will Arise!

Róisín

Róisín – you're the bright one,
You're the right one for me -
We can walk hand in hand?
Down to the band stand,
You'll be my beauty queen -
And if I were king, just for one day,
I'd sit you right next to me -
In a crown made of gold,
You'll never grow old,
You always will be free -

Róisín – you're the top of the walk,
The brightest star in the sky -
You're the waves of the sea,
The wind that blows free,
The apple of my eye -
But oh, you're the mad one,
You're the sad one,
Who's walking this world all alone -
So come take my hand,
We'll dance with the band,
And then I'll take you home -

Róisín - you are beautiful,
More beauty I've never seen -
From the top of the land, to the silvery sand,
Nor any where's between -
So just grab your hat and put on your coat,
And we'll we go walk in the rain -
I'll light up a smoke and then crack a joke,
Just to see you smile - Róisín –

Róisín – I have seen,
This world has let you down -
And if I could, you know that I would,
Change it all around -
Róisín - I have seen,
You're longing for yesterday -
And I'd take your hand, all over this land,
But you're many miles away ...

GOD BLESS WOMAN

God Bless Woman,
The eternal mystery,
The Goddess of the sky,
The Star upon the sea –

The light upon the darkness,
The beacon in the night,
The walker of the many paths,
Showing the way that's right -

The witch upon the beach,
Barefoot upon the sand,
The wise-woman from yesteryear,
Who walks upon the land -
The Queen of the forest,
Cast spells amongst the trees,
And long ago I lost,
When she cast a spell on me -

God Bless Woman,
And all she gives to man,
To make her walk 3 steps behind,
Was not part of the plan -
To love them all this much,
Surely is a crime?
If so I'm charged and guilty,
And the wonder was all mine -

God Bless Woman, The eternal mystery,
The Goddess of the sky, The Star upon the sea –

THE LAST KING OF CAMELOT

The last King of Camelot,
Sailed upon the breeze -
As his coffin moved through silent streets,
The world fell on its knees -

The stars fell down from the sky,
With a ghostly hollow shrill,
November twenty-second,
the day the Earth stood still -

Elm Street was a nightmare,
To sleep, perchance to dream -
And wonder upon what was lost,
and what could have, might have been -

A patsy at the window,
A magic bullet was the cause,
With Jack's Ruby slippers,
We're off to the land of Oz -

While fingers pointed all around,
The patsy got the blame -
But the killers swiftly slipped away,
To them it's all a game -

Hiding in plain sight they say,
In a bush or in a tree -
By skull and bones, a game of thrones,
By the water's gate times three –

Give them bread and circuses,
And a mop-top song to sing -
Feed them dope and sex and television,
And a dream on which to cling -

But the dreamer of our dreams is dead,
We shan't forget his name -
And since he passed away, you'll see,
Nothing is the same -

That white picket fence has fallen,
It's stripes are fading fast -
While a puppet king sits on the throne,
Another that won't last -

Imposters they will come and go,
Forget them, forget them not -
But none are fit to lace his shoes,
The true King of Camelot!

Scotia 2016

Scotia stands upon the cusp,
Of anither election day -
We'll have to go along with it,
Whatever, come what may –

To vote or not, for the same old lot,
When will real change come to be?
Vote yellow, green or in-between,
And every colour you can see –

Predictions they will come and go,
And the pollsters never tire -
Your votes and faith, they want them baith,
For the brand new tartan messiah –

It runs so deep, but her privy keeps,
With Murdoch & auld Lizzy too -
She'll bring brand new homes in fracking zones,
And a named person for me & you –

So listen well, to what I tell,
And think it for yourself -
There's no disguise, as foodbanks rise,
What happened to Scotia's wealth?

Who'll lose the most, in postal votes,
Who'll stitch it up so well?
When you're out of luck & fracked tae f*ck,
Too late, you'll be in Hell!

So before ye go, down to the Polls,
Think before you talk,
Whatever ye do, will come back to you,
We've a lang, lang, way to walk –

Another 4 years, of sweat & tears,
And still no indie-ref -
Beneath Big Ben, at number ten,
There's a man who's f*cking deaf!

In 2019, beneath the queen,
Will he stay or will he go?
Before he does, let's all of us,
Let him hear a Lion roar!

VIEW FROM AN IRISH BAR IN SCOTLAND

The Irish bar is full o' stars,

But most of them are Brits,

They think they're wide and awfy snide,

They just get on my teats –

So take a guess, I voted YES,

They're choking on their beer,

They roll their eyes, just mystified,

They're full o' Christmas cheer –

They round in packs, the Union Jacks,

They're here for sports TV,

For Scotland's fare, they could'nae care,

That's fir the likes o' me –

They like their songs and nuclear bombs,

Mixed with austerity –

The flutes and drums, the long range guns,

Rule Britannia can't you see?

So Scots Wha Hae, nae mare tae say,

Let's leave it for one day,

Bar wish ye well, nae mair tae tell,

See ye later in Noo Year!

TELL ME WHY YOU TOOK THE SOUP?

Tell me why, I'd like to know,
Of your bloodlines from so long ago -
A name once so proud and true,
Tell me what that means to you?

Do you know where it all begins?
Of your clansmen,
And your kith and kin -
Stories to tell and songs to sing,
To forget them now would be a sin -

You've turned your back,
On all those days,
Disowned and shrugged,
And shunned their ways -
Ancestors turn within their graves,
As you embrace the power knaves -

Does the soup taste good,
Did you get a roll?
Like a Judas undercover mole -
But even if you're on the dole,
It's no excuse to sell your soul -

I'll tell you now and it is no joke,
I really hope you feckin' choke -
As just how low can you stoop?
Tell me why you took the soup?

POOR WEE EFFIE MacGAEL

Wee Effie MacGael,

Reads the Daily Fail –

They scared her half to death,

Saying her pension was bereft -

She almost voted Yes,

'Til she read about the mess -

The papers said was next,

If Scotland walked out & left -

The union she was better in,

To leave would be a sin -

The banks were closing down,

And moving out of town -

The prices they would rise,

In the supermarkets sky high -

She'd probably starve to death,

If Scotland voted Yes -

If the cold didn'ae get her first,

They'd switch her heating aff -

Her bus pass would expire,

In a Scottish funeral pyre -

She'd be mugged upon the streets,

By any nationalist she meets -

She's sitting waiting now,

Patiently for the Vow -

To be delivered soon,

By dear old Gordon Broon -

But the odds are looking dire,

The time surely has expired -

He couldnae be a liar?

Swimming in a Better Together quagmire -

Poor Wee Effie MacGael,

She read the Daily Fail -

It's not her fault you see,

She didn't have goog - el or a PC -

God Bless her broken heart,

We knew it from the start,

And that's the end of this tale,

Of poor wee Effie MacGael.

THE ELFIN QUEEN

Elfin Queen, Oh Elfin Queen,
Tell me now, where have you been?
Between the worlds or in a dream?
Will ye ne'er come back, oh Elfin Queen?

Lips like cherry, skin like snow,
The sweetest changeling I could know,
Forever young, but somehow old,
Her love's not bought, and never sold -

She dances now across the moon,
On forest floor and all too soon,
I lose myself within her tune,
From midnight past, until the noon -

She leads me here, she leads me there,
Through faery glens and meadows fair,
And down inside the mountains bare,
Past dragon's den, she whispers there -

And down beneath in darkened halls,
Strange music echoes off the walls,
Her people laugh and proudly play,
Their Elfin songs, 'til break of day -

We dance and drink and dance some more,
In circles deep, as fire roars,
She takes my hand and holds my gaze,
And leads me off, my heart ablaze –

On bed of straw, in some quiet place,
She lays me down, my pulse does race,
She tells me now - "Your turn to gaze,"
As we start the dance, that ends the chase -

My heart on hers, her lips on mine,
Amongst the vines, our limbs entwined,
Between the rhythm and the rhyme,
She crowns me King, of another time -

And in the morn, when I awake,
The blackbird calls another day,
Though she is gone a long, long way,
She's left a note, and it says -

"Elfin Queen, Oh Elfin Queen,
Tell me now, where have you been?
Between the worlds, or in a dream?
Will ye ne'er come back, oh Elfin Queen?"

I DON'T OWN SCOTIA, BUT SCOTIA OWNS ME

There's no tartan messiah to be seen,
We only have ourselves to live that dream -
You won't find it on the arse of the German Queen,
Or by looking back at what-could-have, might-have-
been -

All we want is our people to be free -
I don't own Scotia, but Scotia owns me.
All we want is our nation's sovereignty,
I don't own Scotia, but Scotia owns me.

There's no Scottish Central Bank to be seen,
We only have ourselves to live that dream -
For the politicians aren't all that they seem,
And their promises of what-could-have, might-have-
been -

All we want is our people to be free -
I don't own Scotia, but Scotia owns me.
All we want is our nation's sovereignty,
I don't own Scotia, but Scotia owns me.

There's no indieref2 to be seen,
We only have ourselves to live that dream -
Soundbites, scripts and logos fall like sand,
But we'll walk the road to freedom hand-in-hand -

All we want is our people to be free -
I don't own Scotia, but Scotia owns me.
All we want is our nation's sovereignty,
I don't own Scotia, but Scotia owns me.

THE 99% PARTY

The Electoral Commission,
Has made a decision,
The 99% Party,
Is finally out of remission -

Almost rejected,
Due to May's snap election,
And any final changes,
Were right out of the question -

Do we stand for Scottish Yes?
Of course we bloody do,
We stand for Yes in England,
And Yes in Wales too -

So break up the union,
Smash it all to bits,
Then come back together,
Using only our combined wits -

A voluntary Council of the Isles,
That's the way to go,
No Monarchy Queen, to be seen,
The people run the show -

But while we're stuck together,
There's lots that we can do,
For citizens' rights, with all our might,
That's up to me and you -

No 1% Elite,
Working behind the scenes,
We'll chase them out of politics,
And shelf them with the Queen!

FREEDOM

Freedom from debt, slavery & all,
We must free ourselves, fight or fall -
Freedom from extremist's, doctrine ingrained,
It's enough brainwashing to declare you insane –

Freedom from the cronyist, nepotist set,
When the 99 wake up, that's a sure fire bet -
Freedom from sectarian, religious divide,
The holes in their stories are ten miles wide –

Freedom from the bankers and crooks wearing ties,
When we burst the world bank for living a lie -
Freedom from the frackers, they're absolute crackers,
Goodbye to them and their Tory backers –

Freedom from dress codes and the fashion police,
And absentee landlords who shirk on a lease -
Freedom from the media and state TV,
Just spread the news around between you & me –

Freedom from the fascists and their master race,
The dividers and conquerors that are in your face -
Freedom from the stereo, typical gender roles,
Yin and yang balance is a higher goal –

Freedom from privileged 1% rule,
If you can't f*cking see it, you're playing the fool -
Freedom from social status inequality,
Replace that with democratic meritocracy –

Freedom from within, through the noise and din,
To know thyself is not a sin -
Freedom from these things would be fine enthralled,
But freedom from monarchy would be best of all!

Glossary of Terms:

Scots - English

aboot – about / aff – off / ain – own / anither – another / arse – ass / 'aw – all / awfy – awful / baith – both / cannae – cannot / claes – clothes / daeing – doing / didnae - didn't / doon – down / feart – afraid / fir – for / hae – have / hame – home / hiv – have / indieref2 - 2nd independence referendum / isnae - isn't / jaked – drunk / lang – long / mair – more / metter – matter / naw - no noo – now / oor – our / oot – out / roond – round / toon – town / Scotia – Scotland / sleekit - sly, cunning, shady / tae – to / tak – talk / wance – once / we'an – Child / wha – who / wi' – with / wid – would / wisnae - wasn't / ye – you / yer – your / yin – one /

About The Author:

S.G. (Seána Geri) McCloskey is a transgender (male to female) author, poet, activist and single parent. She lives with her children on Scotland's west coast.

Published Works:

Citizens Not Slaves: The Rise of the 99%

Blood On The Butcher's Apron

Róisín & Other Poems

Riggederendum Blues

Poetry of the 99%

Official Author Website:

sgmccloskey.com